Hei

The T   cury

Edith Girvan
Series editor: Jim McGonigle

Heinemann Educational Publishers
Halley Court, Jordan Hill, Oxford, OX2 8EJ
a division of Reed Educational & Professional Publishing Ltd

Heinemann is a registered trademark of Reed Educational & Professional Publishing Ltd

OXFORD MELBOURNE AUCKLAND
JOHANNESBURG BLANTYRE GABORONE
IBADAN PORTSMOUTH NH (USA) CHICAGO

© Edith Girvan 2002

First published 2002

ISBN 0 435 32093 9
04 03 02
10 9 8 7 6 5 4 3 2 1

Designed and typeset by Ken Vail Graphic Design, Cambridge

Illustrated by Linda Rogers Associates (Jim Eldridge).

Printed and bound in the United Kingdom by Bath Colourbooks

Picture research by Frances Topp

Photographic acknowledgements

The author and publisher would like to thank the following for permission to reproduce photographs:
Advertising Archive: 27B; AP/Topham: 55D, 55E; Corbis/Bettmann: 4A, 50H; Corbis: 48E; Hulton Archive: 10G, 15C, 28C (right), 29D, 30E, 34C, 37A, 38 (all), 40C, 44F, 47D, 54C; MEPL: 5C (both), 18A, 23F; National Museum of Labour History: 25A (both), 28C (left); Popperfoto/Reuters: 61A, 64; Popperfoto: 581; The Scotsman Publications: 63C; Topham/PA: 61B; Topham: 20C, 46A; University of Liverpool Library: 6A, 7D, 8E

Cover photograph © Sotheby's Picture Library

Written source acknowledgements

The authors and publisher gratefully acknowledge the following publications from which written sources in the book are drawn. In some sources the wording or sentence structure has been simplified.

Erich Maria Remarque *All quiet on the Western Front* (Mayflower, 1974): 16D
Nelson Mandela *Long walk to freedom: the autobiography of Nelson Mandela* (Abacus, 1995): 58H

Tel: 01865 888058 www.heinemann.co.uk

Contents

1 A new century

One minute past midnight on 1 January 1900 saw the end of an era and the start of a new age – the twentieth century had arrived. Crowds celebrated the coming of a new century, not knowing what it would bring to them and their families.

◀ *Wealthy Americans prepare to welcome in the new century in New York, just before midnight 31 December 1899.*

In 1901 Queen Victoria died and her son Edward VII became king. The new king and the new century marked the start of change for everyone.

Life in the early twentieth century

At the beginning of the twentieth century life was very different from that of today. Class played a very important role in society and most people came from one of the following three classes:

- Upper class.
- Middle class.
- Working class.

Each person belonged to one particular class and accepted his or her position in society. The richest people belonged to the upper classes and the poorest to the working classes. In terms of numbers the fewest people belonged to the upper classes and the most to the working classes.

The upper classes, also known as 'the aristocracy', were wealthy and could afford to travel and enjoy life in luxury. Most of them owned land or buildings and had large sums of money. They often did not need to work; they could live off their wealth. They entertained and had household servants to do the chores. The children of wealthy families were treated differently depending on whether they were boys or girls. Girls were taught at home by governesses and boys were sent to boarding school. After completing their education, boys could do as they pleased, as there was no need for them to work.

Those who did feel they wanted to work often joined the army or navy, or entered Parliament or the family business. Girls were educated for married life and spent much of their time socialising and attending balls in order to meet a suitable partner for marriage.

The middle classes included rich factory owners, doctors, lawyers and clerks – people who worked with their heads rather than their hands. The middle classes also had servants in their houses although not as many as the upper classes.

The working classes worked for long hours in places such as factories, coal mines, farms and shipyards for little money. In 1901 almost two million working-class women worked as servants for the upper classes. Many working-class people lived in poverty; whole families lived in one room with no inside toilet. If they lost their jobs or were sick they had no income. It was not an easy life being poor in the early 1900s. Seebohm Rowntree carried out an investigation into poverty in York, and the results were very surprising (see Source B).

Source B

That in this land of abounding wealth probably more than a fourth of the population are living in poverty.

Extract from Seebohm Rowntree's investigation into poverty in York, 1901.

Source C

Two families from the early twentieth century.

Questions

1. Read Source B and explain in your own words what Rowntree is saying about the number of poor people in Britain at the time of his investigation.

2. **a.** Match the photographs in Source C with the correct class.
   b. Write a sentence describing the people in each photo and why you think they belong to the class you chose in part **a**.
   c. Write a sentence describing the life each class of people would lead.

Extended writing

1. Write a paragraph explaining what you would do to improve things for the poor in the early twentieth century. Comment on their wages and housing, and what you could do if they lost their jobs or became sick. Add anything else you think you could do to improve life for them.

5

2 The Lusitania

In the early twentieth century many working-class men were involved in the shipbuilding industries in Clydebank (in western Scotland). Working in the shipyards was not an easy life; men worked long hours for low wages. The work was dangerous as workers had to crawl into confined spaces or climb scaffolding to reach the highest parts of the ship.

In 1905 one of the most famous ships was built, the RMS (Royal Mail Ship) *Lusitania*. This ship was ordered by the shipping company Cunard, and was built to challenge the White Star Company in their bid to cross the Atlantic in the fastest time. The *Lusitania* was built at John Brown's shipyards in Clydebank by working-class men, designed and engineered by the middle classes and owned by the upper-class-run Cunard. The *Lusitania* was ready to set off on its maiden voyage from Southampton to New York in September 1907. Over 200,000 people gathered to watch the ship depart.

Source A

▲ *The* **Lusitania** *in John Brown's shipyards in Clydebank, 1907.*

Source B

In splendid sunshine and in the sight of hundreds of spectators both inside and outside the Clydebank yard the *Lusitania* was sent off her stocks at 12.30 o'clock. The naming ceremony was performed by Mary, Lady Inverclyde.

An extract from **The Shipbuilder, October 1906.**

Source C

She is a veritable greyhound of the seas ... a worthy tribute to her lineage.

An extract from **The Times newspaper, September 1907, on the maiden voyage of RMS Lusitania.**

Life on the Lusitania

The *Lusitania* was the largest passenger ship built at the time. It had seven passenger decks which were used for games, walking and getting some fresh air. The ship was also extremely fast, with steam turbines driving four huge propellers.

Life on board the *Lusitania* reflected the way society was divided, being composed of first class, second class and steerage passengers. The first-class passengers were the aristocracy; they had paid for comfort and enjoyed it. These passengers included millionaires who would have stayed in the finest cabins on board. First-class passengers would dine in splendid dining halls with plenty of waiters to serve them. Entertainment would be provided for them – they would attend balls and dances in the evenings and might attend classes or play games during the day.

Second-class passenger accommodation was not quite as sumptuous and involved sharing a cabin and public sitting room (Source D). Second-class passengers would also dine well and be entertained, but they were excluded from the very fine privileges that the first-class passengers enjoyed.

The third-class or steerage passengers shared cabins and their rooms were the smallest on board (Source E). These passengers were not allowed to enter certain areas inside the ship or on deck – these were reserved for second- and first-class passengers. They would have their meals in large canteens and would often provide their own entertainment by playing musical instruments and dancing. Their berths were usually in the lowest parts of the ship.

Source D

Second-class accommodation on the **Lusitania.** ▶

Source E

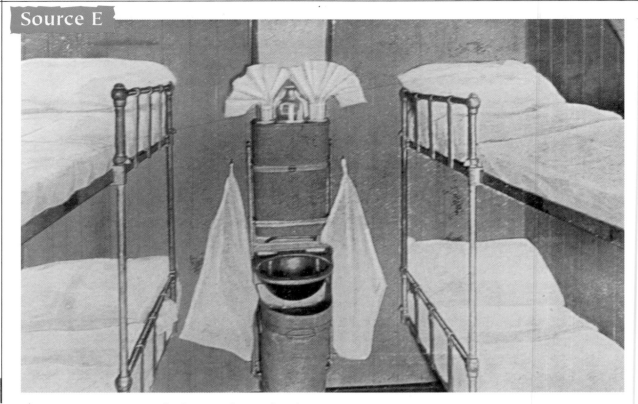

▲ *Steerage accommodation on the* Lusitania.

The *Lusitania* had a sister ship (a ship built by the same company and in a very similar style) called RMS *Mauretania*. This ship sailed on its maiden voyage in November 1907, a month after the *Lusitania*. The construction of the two ships had been paid for by large loans from the British government. In return for these loans, the British Navy claimed the right to use the *Lusitania* or the *Mauretania* in time of war.

In August 1914, almost seven years after the maiden voyages of both ships, the First World War broke out. The *Lusitania* and the *Mauretania* were officially taken over by the navy for war duties. However, only the *Mauretania* was actually used by the navy, so the *Lusitania* continued its regular transatlantic passenger services.

Questions

1. Explain the role of each class of people in the building of the *Lusitania*.

2. Look at the following list of jobs carried out in the shipyards. Choose any three and try to find out what the work involved.

   - Foremen.
   - Riggers.
   - Platers.
   - Shipsmiths.
   - Brassfinishers.
   - Sheet ironworkers.
   - French polishers.
   - Tinsmiths.
   - Shipwrights.
   - Joiners.

3. Which social class do you think was involved in the naming ceremony?

4. Where do you think the workers would have been on launching day?

5. What does the quote from *The Times* (Source C) tell us about the speed of the *Lusitania*? Explain your answer.

6. List as many differences as you can between the first-class and steerage passengers on the *Lusitania*.

Extended writing

1. Imagine you are Lady Inverclyde (Source B). Write what you would say when naming the *Lusitania*. You will need to mention where you are, which company built the ship and the name of the ship.

2. Design a sales package to sell tickets for a journey on the *Lusitania*. Your package should include a brochure, ticket and poster. Make your brochure in a booklet form with diagrams as well as information about the ship. The tickets should reflect the luxury of the ship and include prices and arrival/departure times. The poster would be colourful and fully explain the magnificence of the ship.

The sinking of the Lusitania

On 1 May 1915, the *Lusitania* left New York, bound for Liverpool. As the USA was not involved in the First World War at this time, and the ship was carrying many American passengers, few people were concerned about the possibility of attack by German submarines. This was in spite of a notice (see Source F) posted by the German Embassy in the USA, which appeared directly underneath a poster advertising the crossing.

On Friday 7 May the *Lusitania* reached the war zone (the area of sea around Britain), in which enemy submarines might be expected. The ship's captain, William Turner, took some precautions against attack. He ordered all the lifeboats to be swung out, all look-outs to be doubled and high speeds to be maintained.

Source F

Notice!

Travellers intending to embark on the Atlantic voyage are reminded that a state of war exists between Germany and her allies and Great Britain and her allies; that the zone of war includes the waters adjacent to the British Isles; that, in accordance with formal notice given by the Imperial German Government, vessels flying the flag of Great Britain, or any of its allies, are liable to destruction in those waters and that travellers sailing in the war zone on ships of Great Britain or her allies do so at their own risk.

**Imperial German Embassy
Washington, D. C., 22 April 1915**

The notice from the German Embassy in the USA.

9

At 2.15pm, just after the passengers had finished lunch, Captain Turner heard an officer, Leslie Morton, shout, 'There is a torpedo coming, Sir'. The alarm was sounded but immediately afterwards the torpedo struck the ship before anything could be done. A second explosion came within seconds. Suddenly the ship began to list so severely that the officers could not swing the lifeboats clear of the ship. Panic set in among the passengers and many jumped. The *Lusitania* sank bow first, and in about 20 minutes it had disappeared, with the loss of 1198 lives, including 128 Americans. Only 764 people survived. The bodies of 289 people were recovered from the sea. Only eight of the 22 wooden lifeboats had been launched.

Source G

▲ *An artist's impression of the* Lusitania *sinking, 7 May 1915.*

The German submarine which launched the torpedo was commanded by Captain Schwieger. His mission was to seek and destroy enemy vessels around Britain's coastline. On 7 May he decided to travel back towards Germany, as fuel was getting low. He was patrolling in the Irish Channel when he saw the *Lusitania*. When the ship was within firing range he fired.

Source I

The superstructure above the point of impact and the bridge were torn apart, fire broke out and smoke enveloped the high bridge. The ship stopped immediately and keeled over quickly. It appeared as if the ship was going to capsize very shortly. There was great confusion on board; the boats were made ready and some of them were lowered into the water. Great panic must have reigned. It seemed as if the vessel would be afloat for only a short time. I could not fire a second torpedo into this throng of humanity attempting to save themselves.

From Captain Schwieger's log, 7 May 1915.

Source H

My father and I had just come out of the dining room after lunching and were strolling into the lift on D deck. There was a dull, thud-like, not very loud but unmistakably clear explosion. As I ran upstairs the boat was already keeling over. I went onto A deck. Just after I reached the deck a team of steerage passengers came rushing up and fought their way into the boat nearest us, which was being lowered. They were white faced and terrified. I think they were shrieking, there was no kind of order. They rushed a boat before it was ready for them. It was impossible to lower any more from our side owing to the list on the ship. The ship sank and I was sucked right down with it.

When I came to the surface, I found I had formed part of a large round floating island composed of people and debris of all sorts, lying so close together that at first there was not much water noticeable between them. People, boats, hencoops, chairs, rafts, boards and goodness know what else besides all floating...

Viscountess Rhondda's account of the sinking of the Lusitania.

Newspapers of the world reacted in different ways. The articles in Sources J and K appeared in May 1915.

Source J

Germany must have surely gone mad. It was well known to the German authorities that there were many Americans aboard. The torpedoing and sinking of the *Lusitania* shows a reckless disregard of the opinions of the world in general and of this country in particular – a determination to win war by any means and at all cost.

It is true that Germany threatened to do this very thing but it is also true that when the threat was received Washington met it with the declaration that for every American life taken, the Berlin government would be held to strict account.

From an article in a newspaper, 8 May 1915.

Source K

Last week we predicted the fate that has overtaken the *Lusitania*. Now today we make another prediction. Every large passenger ship bound for Britain is carrying vast quantities of ammunition and explosives of every description. An arsenal whether on sea or on land is not a safe place for anyone.

Much as we regret the staggering loss of life in the disaster that startled the world the facts in the case absolutely justify the actions of the Germans.

From an article in **The Fatherland,** *published on 19 May 1915.*

Although the USA did not immediately declare war on Germany following the sinking of the Lusitania, the sinking greatly affected the opinions of many Americans. Gradually, the tide of public opinion in the USA was turning against Germany. The USA eventually joined the war on the side of the British, French and Russians in April 1917. The fresh troops, which the USA sent to the Western Front, and the increased amount of weaponry certainly played a part in helping the Allies win the war.

Questions

1. Why do you think the German Embassy published the warning? (Source F)

2. **a.** The *Lusitania* took only 20 minutes to sink. What evidence is there in Viscountess Rhondda's account (Source H) which would back this up?
   b. Why is her account of events particularly useful in telling us what happened on board the ship after the torpedo hit?

3. Imagine you were on board the *Lusitania* in May 1915. Write a letter to friends in the USA telling them about the last journey of the *Lusitania*, from the moment you went on board until you arrived safely in Ireland. In your letter give details about your accommodation and your experiences as well as details about the last fateful day.

4. **a.** Read Source J. Using quotes as evidence, what makes it likely that this article appeared in a British newspaper?
   b. According to this report, how did the Americans react to the German warning?

5. **a.** Read Source K. In which country do you think *The Fatherland* was published? Explain your answer.
   b. What allegation about the *Lusitania* is contained in this article?

Extended writing

1. Read the text about the sinking of the *Lusitania*. Now carefully read Sources I and K. What conclusions might you draw about the cargo of the *Lusitania* and Germany's justifications for sinking the ship?

The First World War

On 4 August 1914 Britain declared war on Germany. The declaration of war was greeted with celebrations and people were confident that the war would be over by Christmas. They were very wrong, however, as the declaration was to mark the start of a four-year struggle and to result in the loss of millions of lives. In 1914 Europe was divided into two armed camps.

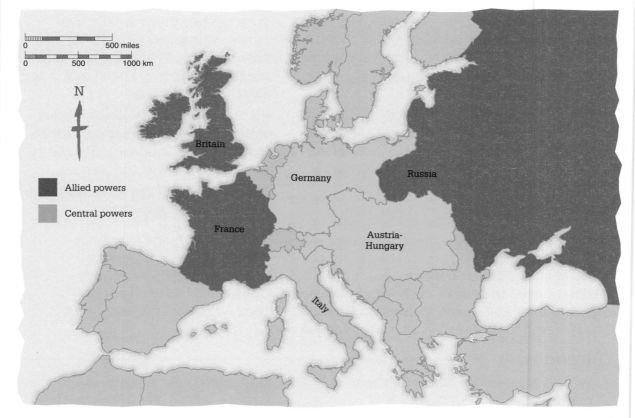

A map of Europe in 1914 showing the two opposing sides in the First World War.

The Home Front

This war was very different from any war that had taken place before. The whole country was involved in the war effort, men and women alike. If Britain was to succeed in winning the war, what happened at home was going to be just as important as the fighting in Europe. The life and work in Britain during the war is known as the Home Front. The fighting troops needed uniforms, weapons and food to keep fighting – so industry in Britain had to adapt to produce these goods to help the war effort. Factories concentrated on making ammunition and other essential supplies. The government passed new laws to make sure that the war was properly organised.

Government at war

The Defence of the Realm Act (DORA) allowed the government to introduce laws to protect the people of Britain and to prevent German spies from gaining information about British tactics in the war. DORA resulted in the following:

- Cutting down or destroying bridges or telegraph wires was forbidden.
- Talking on telephones in a foreign language was forbidden.
- Permission was needed to buy binoculars.
- Pub opening hours were cut down and beer was watered down to reduce drunkenness.
- Newspapers were censored.

Rationing

As the war progressed, fighting at sea increased. This caused food to become scarce in Britain, as by 1914 much of this was imported from other countries. Ships carrying imports had difficulty in reaching Britain, leaving it isolated and cut off. The British people therefore had to try to produce as much of their own food as possible. This was a very important part of the war effort – while the army was making progress in Europe, the people at home could not be left to starve. Indeed, these people were needed to make munitions for the army to use against the enemy. As so many men had been enlisted to fight, the job of farming the land to produce more food fell to women. Many of them became involved in farming, and were sent to live and work on farms all over Britain.

Even with the extra effort put into farming the land, food supplies were short. The government had to do something to try to make the most of the food that was available. In 1916 the Ministry of Food was set up to try to control food supplies. It did this by introducing rationing.

Ration books were issued to every person. Each book contained a certain number of coupons for different items of food, to be used over a certain period of time. This meant that the food was to be distributed equally between people and regularly over time.

Joining up

In 1914, at the start of the First World War, men in Britain were enthusiastic about joining the armed forces and fighting the enemy. They were keen to fight for 'King and Country', and over 400,000 volunteers signed up in the first month. They had many reasons for joining up. Young men wanted adventure, the chance to see another part of the world, and to meet other people. Some joined simply because their friends did. In Glasgow, volunteers marched through the streets singing. They did not realise how long the war would last, or how bad the conditions would be.

However, as the war progressed and terrible stories of the fighting and the casualties reached home, fewer and fewer men were keen to join up. Ways of trying to encourage men to join up appeared all over Britain. Posters on walls and advertisements in newspapers helped to persuade some men to join up. Songs sung in local music halls also played a part.

A poster used to encourage men to fight in the First World War. ▶

In 1916, as so many men had been killed or injured and fewer were volunteering to join up, the government introduced conscription (compulsory military service). At first only single men were required to join up, but then married men were called on as well. Some men were exempt from conscription – these included men doing essential work in Britain (for example engine drivers or doctors) or men deemed unfit. Some men simply refused to join up for moral reasons. These men were known as conscientious objectors and were often called to tribunals to convince the authorities that they should not be forced to fight. Many of them helped the war effort in different ways, for example acting as stretcher-bearers or ambulance-men at the front.

Source A

Daddy, what did YOU do in the Great War ?

Questions

1. Look at the list of measures that DORA allowed the government to introduce. Explain how each of these might have helped protect the people of Britain and prevent German spies from gaining information.

2. **a.** Why was rationing introduced?
   b. How did rationing help the war effort?

3. **a.** Look at Source A. How might this help persuade men to join up?
   b. Read Source B. What words in the song might help persuade men to join up?
   c. Why were women usually used to sing this type of song?
   d. Explain why the government had to introduce conscription.

Source B

We've watched you playing cricket
And every kind of game:
At football, golf and polo
You men have made your name.
But now your country calls you,
We shall love you all the more.
So come and join the forces
As your fathers did before.
Oh we don't want to lose you
But we think you ought to go,
For your King and your Country,
Both need you so.
We shall want you and miss you,
But with all our might and main
We cheer you, thank you, kiss you
When you come back again.

A poem written to encourage men to join up.

14

Fighting in Europe

The methods of fighting were also different from what had gone before. Progress in science and technology meant that weapons were now much more efficient and could inflict more damage on the enemy. The armies of 1914 had to dig trenches to protect themselves from attack. These trenches were protected with sandbags and barbed wire.

Life in the trenches was difficult; it was noisy, dirty, dangerous and extremely unpleasant. A trench was about 2 metres deep and water would gather along the bottom. Standing in water for long periods sometimes led to a painful infection called 'trench foot'. The trench was where men had to live, sleep, eat and hopefully survive for several weeks on end. Behind the front line trenches were support trenches and behind these were reserve trenches. Trenches were built in zig-zags, to prevent the enemy from firing down the line of the trench if it was captured. Men lived in constant fear of being ordered to 'go over the top' in an attack on enemy trenches. The area between the trenches of the fighting sides was known as 'No Man's Land'.

Source C

A British trench in the First World War. ▲

barbed wire

sandbags

firing step

water   duckboards

A diagram of a trench. ▲

Source D

The rats here are particularly repulsive, they are so fat – the kind we call corpse rats. They have shocking evil naked faces and it is nauseating to see their long nude tails ... at last we put a stop to it ... we lay a trap ... we hear the first shuffling ... it is the sound of many little feet ... the torches switch on and every man strikes at the heap which scatters with a rush. The result is good. We toss the bits of rat over the parapet and again lie in wait. Several times we repeat the process. They return no more ... nevertheless before morning the remainder of the bread on the floor has been carried off. In an adjoining sector they [the rats] attacked two large cats and a dog, bit them to death and devoured them.

An extract from the novel **All Quiet on the Western Front** *written by the German novelist Erich Maria Remarque, who fought in the trenches during the war.*

The fighting in the trenches went on until 1918. By this time the Americans had joined the war, mainly because of the sinking of the *Lusitania*. When the war ended in 1918, the effects of it were felt in Europe and the USA for a long time. One of the more positive effects of the war was the change it brought for women.

Questions

1. Look at the map of Europe on page 12. Why do you think Germany, Austria-Hungary and Italy were called the Central Powers?

2. Describe how the war affected everyday life in Britain from 1914 to 1918.

3. Look at the diagram of the trench on page 16 and explain the purpose of each of the following features:

   - Sandbags.
   - Barbed wire.
   - Duckboards.
   - Firing step.

4. Read Source D. Do you think this extract is a useful source for telling us about trench life?

Extended writing

1. a. Imagine you are a soldier fighting in the trenches. Write a letter home to a loved one describing your life there. Mention the noise, the smells, the sights and how you feel about the fighting.
   b. Look at the letter you have just written. During the war you would not have been allowed to send it with this amount of detail. It would have been censored and much of the information cut out.

      - What kind of information do you think would have been cut out?
      - Give two reasons why letters and information sent home would have been censored.

17

4 The role of women in the early twentieth century

One of the most remarkable changes to take place between 1900 and 1920 was the position of women in society. In 1914 Britain was a 'man's' country and women were expected to provide a pleasant home for the men. Girls and boys were educated differently. Girls were largely taught home-making skills while boys were prepared for a working life. Women faced discrimination in many aspects of their lives. When women did work, they were paid lower wages than men even if they were doing the same job.

Education for women was also limited. It had only been in the late nineteenth century that they had been accepted into some universities. However, while women could study and qualify in subjects like law, they could not then go on to practise them, as women were not allowed to enter professions like law and medicine.

Even if not at fault, women were not allowed to divorce their husbands. Most major decisions in the household would be made by men, and all the property in a house, including any children, automatically belonged to the husband. Women did not have the right to vote and so had no way of changing or improving their situation.

The struggle for the right to vote

In order to try to improve their situation, 'votes for women' became the battle cry for many in the early 1900s. Women fighting for the vote became known as Suffragists or Suffragettes as they were fighting for 'suffrage', or the right to vote. The Suffragists used peaceful methods to gain support for their cause. They petitioned Parliament, wrote to MPs and distributed leaflets to try to influence people and bring about change.

Source A

SHE. IT IS TIME I GOT OUT OF THIS PLACE. WHERE SHALL I FIND THE KEY?

CONVICTS AND LUNATICS HAVE NO VOTE FOR PARLIAMENT

Should all Women be classed with these?

A British cartoon, published in 1910, suggesting women should be allowed to vote. ▶

The Suffragettes felt that these peaceful methods were getting nowhere and so resorted to violent means to gain attention. In 1897 the National Union of Women's Suffrage Societies (the NUWSS) was formed. The Women's Social and Political Union (the WSPU) was formed in 1903 and was led by Emmeline Pankhurst and her daughter, Christabel. The Suffragettes, as they became known, broke windows, interrupted Parliament, poured acid on bowling greens and caused major disturbances to try to get attention. The women believed that they were right in their struggle and that using violence was the only way to gain the vote.

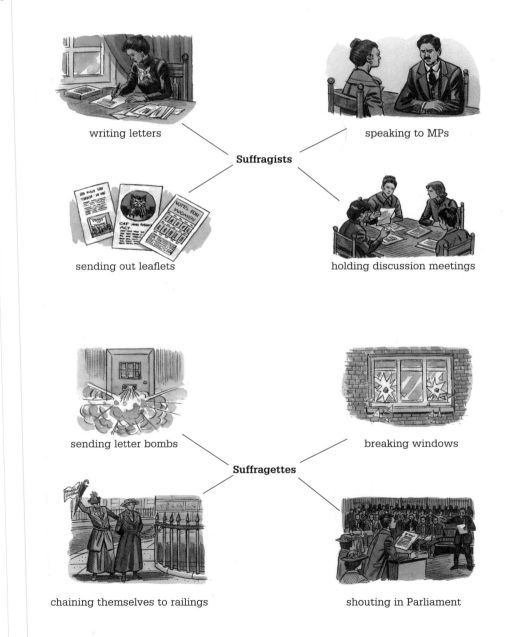

writing letters

speaking to MPs

Suffragists

sending out leaflets

holding discussion meetings

sending letter bombs

breaking windows

Suffragettes

chaining themselves to railings

shouting in Parliament

▲ *The different methods of Suffragists and Suffragettes.*

Following their violent outbreaks, many Suffragettes were arrested and put in jail. This gained them more publicity and to add to this they often went on hunger strikes. The authorities did not want the women to die in jail, so any woman who refused to eat was force-fed (see Source B). Some women suffered permanent damage to their throats and noses from this ordeal, often making them invalids for the rest of their lives. Some of the women who survived hunger strikes were given medals by the Suffragettes.

The brutality of force-feeding led the government to look at other ways of dealing with Suffragettes. In 1913 an act was passed in Parliament which became commonly known as the Cat and Mouse Act because of the way it treated the women. This Act allowed prisoners to be released until they were well. They would then be re-arrested.

Source B

They push a tube up the nostril which goes wriggling down into the stomach, then there's a funnel on the end of the tube they pour the water – pour the food in you see. And all the time they were pushing this tube down, I kept coughing. In almost no time intense pains ... came all around my chest and it was almost impossible to breathe. Well I didn't know what was the matter, but I understood it was double pneumonia and pleurisy, due to food getting into the lung.

A Suffragette describes the experience of force-feeding.

20

Source C

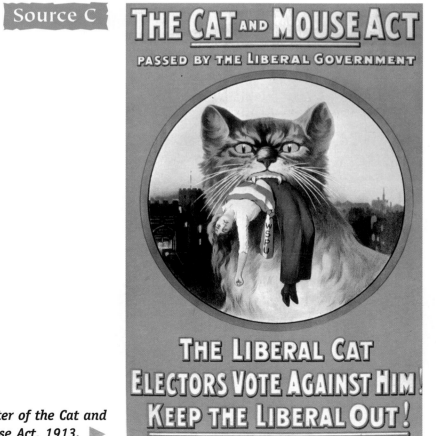

A poster of the Cat and Mouse Act, 1913. ▶

The struggle to obtain the vote for women continued until August 1914 when the Suffragettes and Suffragists decided to put all their efforts into fighting the common enemy – Germany – during the war. The Suffragettes gave up their militancy in favour of the war effort. Instead of the 'Right to Vote', their slogan became the 'Right to Serve'.

Emmeline Pankhurst persuaded the government that women should be allowed to work in munitions factories. By July 1917, 800,000 women were employed in the munitions industry. Women became involved in farming, and took the jobs of men who had joined the armed forces. They worked as drivers, bus conductors, police, railway staff and factory workers. Some women even went to the areas of fighting in Europe and worked as nurses and intelligence officers. Because of the enormous effort of women during the war, the vote was given in 1918 to all women over the age of 30. This was followed ten years later by the vote being extended to all women over the age of 21.

Source D

It is a thousand times more the duty of the militant Suffragettes to fight the Kaiser (German Emperor) for the sake of liberty than it was to fight anti-suffrage governments.

An extract from **The Suffragette, 16 April 1915.**

Questions

1. Look closely at the cartoon in Source A. What does it tell you about the people in Britain who had the right to vote (the suffrage) and those who did not.

2. Which group of campaigning women do you think would be listened to more – the Suffragists or the Suffragettes? Make at least one point to back up your answer.

3. Why do you think the government and the authorities went to such lengths to stop the women dying in jail?

4. The Suffragettes published the poster shown in Source C. Describe what this tells you about the feelings of the Suffragettes towards the Act.

5. What did the Suffragettes do when war was declared, and why did they decide to do this?

Extended writing

1. Write a report in your own words about the struggle to obtain the vote for women. In it you must decide why women got the vote. Your report should examine the role of the Suffragists, the Suffragettes and the war in helping women gain the vote.

— Suffragettes in Scotland

The Suffragettes waged an active campaign all over Britain. News and reports were published in the suffragette journal *Votes for Women*. Many events which took place in Scotland were recorded. In October 1908 an article was published which showed the amount of support given to the Suffragettes (see Source E).

Source E

On Thursday a bill-distributing party went to Paisley, where we were amused to find that many people regarded the calling of a meeting to discuss the question of votes for women as a 'very sensible idea'.

From an article in **Votes for Women, 8 October 1908.**

In October 1909 the first militant demonstrations took place in Glasgow and Dundee. Women in Scotland showed that they could equal the violent protests of their counterparts in England. As the Suffragettes' campaign progressed, Farington Hall in Dundee and Leuchars railway station were burned to the ground. Holyrood Palace in Edinburgh was closed for fear of an attack. One of Scotland's most beautiful churches in East Lothian – Whitekirk – was also burned down. Arresting suspected Suffragettes did not stop the action – if anything it encouraged more attacks.

One of Scotland's leading Suffragettes was a woman called Flora Drummond. She became known as General Drummond because she wore a uniform and led a drum and fife band on marches in London. She was an exciting speaker to listen to and coped well with heckling from the crowd. On one occasion she hired a launch on the River Thames and sailed it close to the House of Commons, so that she could harass a group of MPs who were outside on the terrace. She was imprisoned nine times as a result of her actions. One of her more daring actions occurred in 1906. Fellow Suffragette Irene Miller was arrested for knocking on the door of 10 Downing Street, the home of the Prime Minister, and demanding a reply to her request to see the Prime Minister about the vote for women. While Irene Miller was being arrested, Flora Drummond dodged inside 10 Downing Street. She was caught, however, and was also arrested.

Because of their actions, women like Flora were often sent to jail. Their time in jail was used by many women to give them even more publicity. They did this by going on hunger strike. The first woman to go on hunger strike was a Scottish woman called Marion Wallace Dunlop. She was imprisoned in London, in Holloway Prison. The prison authorities thought the best way to deal with hunger-strikers was to force-feed them (Source F). Perth Prison also used force-feeding tactics on its prisoners. Arabella Scott was held in isolation in Perth Prison for 36 days. In the prison medical notes, there is an entry stating that she was force-fed three times in one day (Source G).

Source F

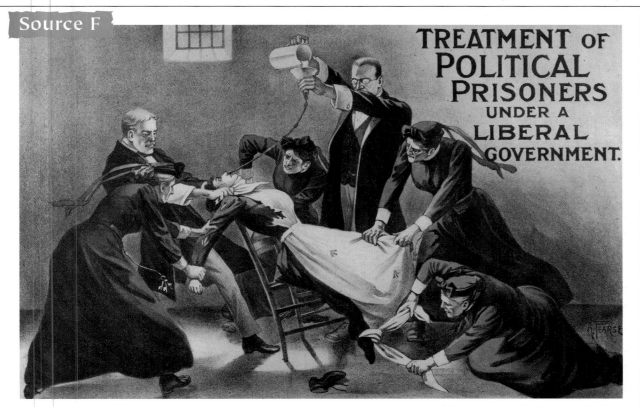

A poster published by the WSPU in 1910, showing a Suffragette being force-fed.

Another influential Suffragette in Scotland was Elsie Inglis. She studied medicine and became a doctor in Edinburgh. In 1901 she established a maternity hospice at Bruntsfield Hospital, and employed only women. She also fought for better healthcare for all women in Scotland. In 1906 Elsie founded the Scottish Women's Suffrage Federation. In 1914, at the start of the First World War, the federation set up the Organisation of Scottish Women's Hospitals. As part of this organisation, she set up hospitals for soldiers in Russia and Serbia.

Questions

1. Explain why the Suffragettes were not afraid to take part in activities which might result in their being arrested.

2. **a.** Look at Source F. In what ways would posters like this help the cause of the Suffragettes?
   b. Explain how posters like this might have damaged the Suffragettes' cause.

3. Imagine you are a Suffragette. What actions might you take part in which would draw attention to your cause and encourage people in Britain to support you?

Source G

On the removal of the gag my head was seized and my chin was dragged upwards and backwards. Sometimes voluntarily, sometimes involuntarily, the food would be returned into my mouth and, unable to escape, would burst through my nose. Then my nose would be pinched and I would be ordered to swallow it again. I wouldn't, and struggled for breath, then they would say, "We will let you breathe when you turn purple".

Arabella Scott's account of being force-fed.

5 The Twenties – unemployment and the trade unions

The end of the war

The end of the First World War in November 1918 brought peace to Europe, but it also brought many problems for people in Britain and Europe.

Women

During the war, women had been encouraged to work in jobs traditionally seen as belonging to men. In these jobs, they were given more responsibility and higher pay than ever before. But in 1918, with soldiers now returning from the war zones in Europe, women were no longer needed in these jobs and were expected to go back to the work they had been doing before the war.

Many women reacted angrily to this. However, there was little they could do, as most people felt that the returning soldiers deserved to have their old jobs back. Two years after the end of the war, there were fewer women employed outside the home than before the war. For the women who were allowed to keep their wartime jobs, it soon became obvious that the men employed to do exactly the same jobs were being paid more money and worked in better conditions.

Perhaps the most important outcome for women was that attitudes were changing. Women had become more confident and men had begun to realise that women deserved to be their equals. Women had more freedom and they celebrated this by wearing short dresses, trousers and short hairstyles. In 1919 women were allowed to enter professions like law or architecture, and in 1921 contraception became available to women for the first time. This meant that women could now have more control over their own lives.

Returning soldiers

When the First World War ended, Prime Minister Lloyd George said that he wanted Britain to be a 'land fit for heroes to live in'. He wanted all the men who had fought in Europe to be considered war heroes, and for them to be treated as such when they arrived back in Britain to carry on with civilian life.

However, the war had cost a huge amount of money. Britain owed the USA £850 million. During the war, Britain had lent £1750 million to Russia. This money was never repaid. The joy and sense of victory felt by the British people after the war soon began to wear off. Men returning from the fighting found that their jobs had been taken on by other people, often women. While a lot of men were given their old jobs back, some found that their jobs no longer existed.

Almost one-third of the men returning from Europe had been badly injured in the fighting. Many had been blinded or had lost arms and legs, others suffered from terrible 'shell-shock' (the memory of the terrible things they had seen or experienced caused them to suffer from extreme stress). These injuries and illnesses meant that they could not take on their old jobs, and they would find it difficult to find new jobs and to settle back into civilian life.

Source A

YESTERDAY-THE TRENCHES

TO-DAY-UNEMPLOYED

Two posters issued by the Labour Party in 1920. ▲

⎯⎯ *Unemployment*

Unemployment began to rise in the early 1920s. In 1921 there were 2.3 million people unemployed. By 1931 this had risen to 3.2 million. There were three main reasons for this increase in unemployment:

- Large numbers of soldiers returning from the war were looking for work at home. This resulted in women losing their jobs.
- The number of jobs in factories decreased as many factories closed down due to a reduced demand for items which had been needed during the war.
- British products were no longer needed for selling overseas to other countries. These countries now had their own industries so did not need to buy goods from Britain. For example, India and Hong Kong were developing their own textile industries, Poland had found more efficient ways to mine coal and Germany was producing more iron and steel.

The effects of unemployment on the job market were great. The more unemployed people there were, the easier it became for employers to try to cut wages and increase working hours. Dissatisfied or unwilling workers were easily replaced.

Questions

1. What do you think the purpose of the posters in Source A was? Explain your answer.

2. Look at the following lists of heads and tails. The heads and tails have been mixed up. Match the correct head with the matching tail so that it makes a sensible comment on the effects of the First World War.

Heads
Soldiers came back from the war
Munitions factories had to close down because
A generation of men had been lost because of

Tails
the army no longer needed so many weapons.
the number of deaths during the war.
to find there were few jobs available for them.

3. Write a paragraph to explain why there was an increase in unemployment by the early 1920s.

New opportunities

In the USA, the 1920s saw a remarkable period of economic activity. American people had money to spend, and American industry was quick to exploit this opportunity. New machines and consumer goods, designed to make everyday life more enjoyable, came crowding on to the market. These included electric vacuum cleaners (named after their inventor, Hoover), the radio and telephone. With extra money in their pockets, American people wanted to enjoy the benefits of this new labour-saving technology.

All of these new inventions had one major requirement – electricity. In Britain, the government saw the opportunity that these new industries offered. Electricity had been available, but only in certain areas. The decision was made to set up a scheme that would cover the whole country, then everybody could buy the latest gadgets to make their life easier. In 1926, the national grid for electricity was established. Pylons were built carrying electric cables all over Britain.

Source B

THE NEW HOOVER CLEANER

Instantly converted for cleaning furniture, draperies, bare floors and linoleum.
Easy to use from floor to ceiling.
Cleans rugs fast and thoroughly.
Keeps rug colors fresh.
Picks up dog hairs, thread and lint.

MORE HOOVER FOR THE MONEY THAN EVER BEFORE. NEW LOW PRICE. SEE YOUR AUTHORIZED HOOVER DEALER FOR DETAILS.

▲ *An advert from the 1930s, showing the new luxury Hoover.*

At first some people were frightened by these new developments but, as they became familiar with them, this fear decreased. For industry in Britain, the national grid was very important. New factories could be set up where the bulk of the population lived. That meant that new consumer industries were established in the Midlands and South of England. Unfortunately, these new industries did not ease the unemployment in the North of England, Scotland and Wales, which still depended on the old industries of the nineteenth century and which remained depressed during this period. Thus, some parts of the country prospered while others still saw high levels of persistent unemployment.

Trade unions

The twentieth century saw a change in trade unions. Trade unions were set up by workers to help improve working conditions, pay and holidays. During the nineteenth century only highly skilled and highly paid craftsmen could join trade unions; they could afford union subscriptions and could bring factories to a standstill if they went on strike. Unskilled workers were not paid very much and were more difficult to organise; union subscriptions were too expensive for them and if they went on strike they could lose their jobs and therefore have no income at all. By the turn of the twentieth century unions for unskilled workers were beginning to appear. The workers soon realised that if they wanted change it would need to be done through their unions. By 1900 the unions had 2 million members.

Trouble came in 1921 in the coal industry when the miners went on strike. Coalmining had been in decline since the war and the mine owners had cut the miners' wages. After striking for one month, in opposition to their pay cuts, the miners returned to work. However the trouble in the mines was not yet over. In 1925 the mine owners decided to increase the working day by one hour and to decrease the miners' wages. The miners did not accept this; they were determined to fight and used the slogan 'Not a minute on the day; not a penny off the pay'.

On Monday 3 May 1926 the miners went on strike again. This time they were joined by workers in other heavy industries, such as transport, iron and steel, electricity and gas. This was a General Strike, and had been called by the Trades Union Congress (TUC). It lasted for nine days and workers throughout the country went on strike.

During the strike newspapers were not able to publish so both the government and the TUC brought out their own papers called *The British Gazette* and *The British Worker*, respectively, which each side used to portray its version of events.

Source C

Two front pages from newspapers at the time of the General Strike. ▲

At first the General Strike was successful, but as the days went on volunteer workers began to do the work of the strikers. At the same time the government tried to stop the strike. On 12 May 1926 the TUC called off the strike as the money for strike pay was running out. Workers returned to their jobs on Monday 17 May.

The miners, however, remained on strike until 30 November 1926, and when they did return they had to work for less money and for longer hours. They had won nothing. In 1927 the Trades Disputes Act made general strikes illegal.

Source D

A worker's demonstration in Crewe, June 1926, during the General Strike. ▲

Trade unions and women

Although the nature of trade unions might have changed, the attitudes of many of the members remained very much the same. This can clearly be seen in their attitude to women. During the nineteenth century unions, like most other sections of Victorian Britain, believed that women should stay at home, looking after their children and keeping their houses tidy. They also believed that women should be ready to serve their husbands when they arrived home from work.

Soon more and more women went out to work. They were among the most exploited group of workers in the country, and they were not allowed to join trade unions. Male union members feared that women would work longer hours for less pay than the men would accept. Also, many of the jobs which had been unionised were skilled jobs, like engineering. Men believed that women were not capable of doing such highly skilled work. Women faced an uphill battle to win recognition from male-dominated trade unions.

Attitudes began to change following the success of the 'Match Girls' strike at the company Bryant and May in 1897, which led to some people boycotting Bryant and May matches. This was the first successful strike by unskilled women in a British industry and led to improvements in pay and better working conditions. It encouraged more women to become union members.

Source E

Some of the Bryant and May 'Match Girls'.

At the start of the First World War, many men volunteered to join the army, leaving factories short of workers. Once more, there was trade union opposition to 'dilution' – where semi-skilled men were allowed to do the jobs previously done only by skilled tradesmen. As the war continued and more men left to fight, the government was forced to accept women working in the factories to replace men. This was on the understanding that, once the fighting was over, the women would make way for the returning soldiers.

Despite the tremendous work which women did during the war, trade unions were still reluctant to accept them as the equal of men. Given the high rates of unemployment during the inter-war period, it is not surprising that men still viewed women as potential rivals for their jobs. Even when they were employed on the factory floor, women were discriminated against in terms of hours of work and rates of pay.

Questions

1. What are trade unions?

2. a. Which industries were involved in the General Strike in 1926?
   b. What effect would a General Strike have on the country?

3. Look at the front pages of the two newspapers from the strike in 1926 (Source C).

   a. Which newspaper do you think was written for the government?
   b. Why do you think both the government and the TUC went to the trouble of writing their own newspapers?

Extended writing

1. Choose one of the main events of the strike and write your own front page of a newspaper to explain the situation on that particular day. Make sure your paper has a name, date, heading and picture to best tell the story of that day.

6

The Thirties – the rise of Hitler

The early 1930s in Britain was a time of depression, with high levels of unemployment and poverty. Life for many people improved in the latter part of the 1930s, with increases in employment and prosperity, but the last two years of the 1930s were overshadowed by the threat of war. That threat came from Germany. Why should Germany threaten the rest of Europe with war so soon after the First World War? There are many reasons for this and to understand them we must begin by looking at what happened in 1918.

The fate of Germany at the end of the First World War. ▲

— The Treaty of Versailles

In January 1919, after the end of the First World War the leaders of the victorious countries (Britain, France and the USA) met at Versailles in France to decide the future of Europe and to try to put together a long-lasting peace. What came out of these meetings was a peace treaty which Germany would sign and promise to uphold.

The treaty dealt only with Germany, and its aim was to prevent such a terrible war from happening again.

● Germany was not involved in the negotiations, but was forced to agree to all the terms.

- Germany was blamed for starting the war. This was covered in the War Guilt Clause (Article 231). By agreeing to this, the Germans were agreeing to accept punishment for starting the war.
- The land in Europe and Africa that Germany had gained before the war was given to other countries. France, Belgium, Denmark, Poland and Lithuania all took land in Europe. Britain, France and South Africa were given German colonies in Africa.
- Military restrictions were placed on Germany's armed forces. No submarines, tanks or aeroplanes were allowed. The size and number of naval ships was limited, and the navy was limited to 15,000 men. Conscription (compulsory military service) was not allowed, and the army was limited to 100,000 men.
- Germany had to pay back huge sums of money (reparations) to the 'winners'. Reparations for the damage caused by the war were set at £6600 million.

Source A

German Delegate Denies War Guilt!

The German delegate said, 'You demand that we should admit that we are the only ones guilty of staring the war. I cannot bring myself to confess to such a monstrous lie. The actions of the German government certainly contributed to the outbreak of war, but we were convinced that our government took these actions to defend our country. I shall never accept that Germany and its people were the only guilty ones'.

An extract from a Scottish newspaper, 1919.

33

The German leaders and German nation were horrified when they learned of the harsh terms of the Treaty of Versailles and called it a 'diktat' (dictated peace). They considered rejecting the treaty but knew this could lead to war. When the German government signed the treaty, it was immediately blamed by the German nation, who claimed they had been 'stabbed in the back' by the government.

The anti-Versailles view such as the one in Source A was held by many Germans and it was exploited by one man in particular – Adolf Hitler. In 1923–4 Adolf Hitler wrote a book which was to influence Germany in the 1930s. His book was called *Mein Kampf* (My Struggle). In it he made four main points:

- Germany must be a great nation again.
- The Treaty of Versailles must be destroyed.
- All Germans must be united under one leader.
- All Jews and communists must be destroyed.

The Germans had been humiliated at Versailles and had to suffer great hardships after the war. In 1923 Germany also suffered from inflation when prices rose more quickly than wages (Source B).

Source B

All the German people knew that a large bank account could not buy a bag of potatoes, a few ounces of coffee or a pound of flour. They knew they were ruined and they could feel the pain of hunger every day.

An extract from an account by an American living in Germany in 1923.

◀ *The effects of inflation in Germany in 1923. Money became worthless.*

34

The rise of Hitler

In 1924 Hitler and the Nazi Party promised the people of Germany what they wanted – power, wealth and freedom. The Germans were desperate and willing to clutch at any new hope that came their way. The 1920s and 1930s saw a huge increase in the number of people who joined the Nazi Party. The effects of inflation, political instability and unemployment had begun to take their toll. Inflation meant people could not afford to buy basic goods. Political instability was making the German people lose faith in the government. With these problems, some businesses closed and unemployment rose. Between 1925 and 1932, unemployment rose from half a million people to six million people. Germany was looking to return to the rest of Europe on equal terms. The Treaty of Versailles had not been fair to the people of Germany and they demanded change. Hitler knew that the people were looking for a scapegoat (someone to blame) for their problems.

By 1933 Hitler had gained power in Germany and was made Chancellor. He quickly banned all other political parties except the Nazi Party. One year later he became Führer (leader) of the country with no political opposition; his word was law.

1933: Germany awakes

What does our Chancellor Hitler want? He wants to lock up communists. He wants Germany to become free of Jews. He wants order and good government. He wants to give every German a job. He wants to help farmers. He wants an army. He wants to make Germany a great nation again.

An extract from a German history textbook published in 1934.

Germany was no longer a democracy but a dictatorship ruled by one person. There was no equality; Hitler ruled by fear, victimising the groups he did not like. He used concentration camps to get rid of thousands of men and women. His actions were mainly against Jews but trade unionists, the handicapped and pacifists faced attack as well.

Consolidating power

Hitler used a number of methods to influence the German people and to 'brainwash' young people. He controlled the newspapers, radio and cinema. In addition to Nazi propaganda Hitler used schools to teach Nazi ideas. In schools, history was used to show German greatness. Young people were encouraged to join Nazi organisations such as the Hitler Youth (for boys) or the League of German Maidens (for girls). These groups gave the Nazis a chance to put across Nazi beliefs to young people and encouraged them to report their parents or teachers if they criticised the Nazi regime. With young people on his side, Hitler had control over many Germans. By the end of the 1930s Germany had gone from being suppressed by the Treaty of Versailles to being ruled by a dictator.

Source E

The new government restored confidence. It reduced the number of unemployed. How? All citizens were expected to work for the Reich. At 18 boys were conscripted into the labour service and then the army. Girls went into farm work or household service. Large scale works such as building Autobahns [motorways] and ammunition factories employed large numbers. Most of the people worked long hours for a wage equal to their previous dole money.

The writings of a visitor to Germany in 1936.

35

Questions

1. Write a paragraph explaining how you think the Germans felt at the end of the First World War.

2. If you were one of the peacemakers in 1918 what would you have done to help Germany and the rest of Europe?

3. How do you think the German people felt about being made to accept responsibility for the war?

4. The article in Source A was printed in Britain. What do you think the British thought of the attitude of the German delegate at the time? Explain your answer.

5. Do you think that the account shown in Source B is an accurate record of what was happening in Germany in 1923? Give reasons for your answer.

6. How did Hitler use the situation in Germany in 1923 to help achieve his ambition of running Germany?

7. Given what Hitler wrote in *Mein Kampf*, who do you think he blamed for the problems in Germany?

8. Source D is an extract from a history textbook used in the 1930s in Germany.

   a. How does it make Hitler and his beliefs look?
   b. Why do you think that German history textbooks were written in this way?

The Second World War and its effects

When Hitler came to power in Germany in the 1930s he started to put some of his policies into action. One of his aims was to regain the land that Germany had lost in 1919 as a result of the Treaty of Versailles. Another aim was to unite the countries of Germany and Austria. By doing this he could unite all German-speaking people under his control. He also wanted to restore arms to the German armed forces, and bring back conscription so that Germany could defend itself.

Although these actions were contrary to the terms that had been agreed in the Treaty of Versailles in 1919, the other countries in Europe ignored them.

German expansion

Hitler began by taking back land. In 1936 he re-introduced German troops into the Rhineland. He then engineered a union with Austria in 1938. This union was called the *Anschluss*. Britain and France did not oppose Hitler's actions as they did not want to start another war, and they believed that the Austrians wanted the union anyway. By 1939 Germany had expanded its territories and was becoming stronger.

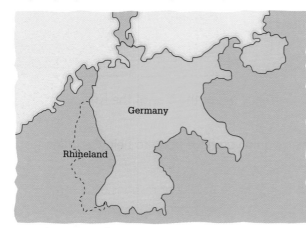

▲ *Germany in 1919.*

▲ *Germany in late 1939.*

War is declared

When Britain's Prime Minister, Neville Chamberlain, discovered what Hitler was doing, he wanted to make sure that any actions taken against Hitler would not lead to war. In Munich in 1938 the two leaders signed an agreement which stated that Britain and Germany would not go to war against each other.

However, in March 1939 Hitler broke one of the terms of the agreement when he occupied Czechoslovakia. This alarmed the leaders of Britain and France, who became concerned that Hitler would invade and take over more countries in Europe. In April 1939 Britain and France promised Poland that they would help defend it against any German invasion. On 1 September 1939 Hitler invaded Poland. Neville Chamberlain's efforts to persuade Hitler to withdraw came to nothing, and Britain declared war on Germany on 3 September 1939.

Preparations for war

When war was declared on Germany, the British people made many preparations to deal with what they felt the main threats to be. People were afraid as they remembered the devastation of the First World War in 1914–18. New technology meant that people in Britain could be attacked by the enemy with gas attacks and bombing raids. They knew this war was going to be different from any other and might involve fighting on British soil. Efforts had to be made to prevent as many people as possible from being killed.

Evacuation

The government decided to move many children and vulnerable people, such as pregnant women and elderly people, out of large cities like London which were likely to be bombed. From 1 to 4 September 1939 around 1.4 million people were evacuated to areas which were not likely to be bombed, usually in the countryside. They went to stay with families who had volunteered to take them in. Children had to live away from their parents and often their brothers and sisters, taking only one suitcase of clothes and possessions with them.

Blackouts and bombing

In 1940 Germany began to carry out bombing raids on Britain. The Germans targeted large towns and cities like London and Coventry. To prevent the German bombers from finding towns during the night, blackouts were organised. All street lamps and external lights were put out. People had to hang thick material in their windows, or paint them black, to stop any light escaping. Using headlights on vehicles was banned. Towns and cities took on a new appearance with black and white painted lamp-posts and kerbs to help people to find their way about during a blackout.

Source A

Council employees painting markings on a London lamp-post, in preparation for blackouts, January 1940.

37

Important buildings were sandbagged to try to prevent damage and houses had sticky tape put on the windows to stop the danger of flying glass. Emergency water tanks were built in public squares. People built air-raid shelters and fled to these whenever the air-raid sirens were sounded. There were two types of shelters – Anderson shelters and Morrison shelters. Anderson shelters were made of corrugated iron and were built outside, usually in people's gardens. Morrison shelters were cages made of wood, with steel mesh sides. These cages were built inside houses, and people would sleep in them or sit inside them during a daylight raid. For people who had no shelter, cellars were used. Many people also started using the underground train stations and tunnels as shelters.

Gas attacks

The government was very concerned that the Germans would drop poisonous gas on to towns and cities in Britain. Every person was issued with a gas mask, and people carried these masks wherever they went. Gas masks became such a large part of everyday life that they began to appear in songs (see Source B).

Rationing

From January 1940 rationing also became part of everyday life. Every family was issued with a ration book which contained coupons for certain foods, for example meat, butter, cheese, tea and eggs. Families could buy only the amount indicated on their coupons. Short supplies meant people often had to queue for food. Families were encouraged to be adventurous with food replacements and substitutes. Powdered eggs and the use of vegetables to replace sugar in baking was common. The aim of rationing was to make sure that food supplies were divided up as equally as possible. In fact, rather than making people hungry, rationing meant that there was enough food available for everyone, and actually helped improve the diet of some people.

Source B

In my wee gas masks, I'm working out a plan
Tho' all the kids imagine that I'm just a bogey man
The girls all smile and bring their friends to see
The nicest lookin' warden in the ARP
Whenever there's a raid on, listen to my cry
An airy-plane, an airy-plane away-way up a kye
Then I run helter-skelter but don't run after me
You'll no get in my shelter for its far too wee.

The ARP was the Air Raid Precaution organisation where volunteers would help make sure people were safe from bomb and gas attacks.

38

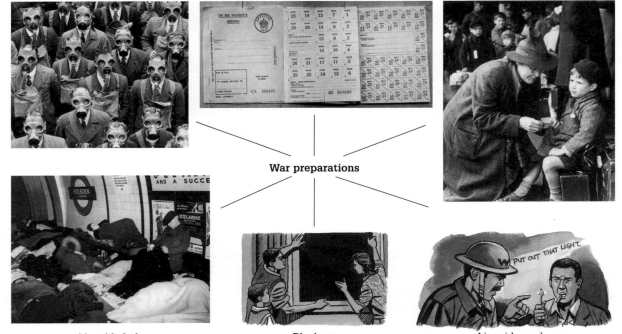

Gas masks

Rationing

Evacuation

War preparations

Air-raid shelters

Blackout

Air-raid wardens

Preparations for war in Britain. ▲

Women in the war

Women had an important part to play in the Second World War. The government realised what a huge part they had played in the First World War, and quickly started a campaign to encourage as many women as possible to work. They were employed in munitions factories, in shipyards and in the transport industry. The Land Army was one of the greatest contributions women made to the war. It was responsible for recruiting, training and placing 'Land Girls' in employment. Land Girls did every type of agricultural and horticultural work, including forestry. On the farms, in factories and in homes the women kept the nation together.

Women were also active on the war front. For instance, Dr Maud Menzies took part in the D-Day Landings in Normandy on 6 June 1944 and some women served overseas helping the resistance in France or in field hospitals as nurses.

Questions

1. Why was the government so concerned about the safety of civilians in Britain, if the fighting was taking place in Europe?

2. Why did the government introduce evacuation?

3. Read Source B. Who do you think this song would appeal to? Give reasons for your answer.

Extended writing

1. Imagine it is Christmas, 1942. War was declared in September 1939. You have seen all of the preparations for war take place. Write a letter to your cousin in the USA. In your letter explain the changes that have taken place which affect you and your family. Explain why these changes have happened and how you and others in your family feel about them.

39

Resistance workers

Between 1939 and 1944 Germany invaded many countries in Europe, including Poland, Austria, Denmark, Norway, Holland, Belgium and France. Many people in these countries did not support Hitler's policies, and formed groups which carried out a secret (underground) war against the Germans. They used various tactics to resist the Germans:

- Some found out about German plans and passed them on to the Allies (the countries fighting against Germany).
- Some helped hide or protect Allied airmen who had been shot down.
- Some helped Jews escape from German-occupied territories.
- Some plotted to kill and bomb Germans or destroy railways or bridges.

The work of these resistance workers was dangerous, and if caught they were killed.

The Holocaust

The Holocaust is the word used for the deliberate murder of over six million Jews in Nazi-occupied Europe. Jewish people in Germany had been persecuted since Hitler came to power in 1933. Hitler thought that the Jews were an inferior race, and that they were a threat to German unity and strength. He began a campaign against the Jews which intensified during the Second World War. Initially, in April 1933, Jewish shops and businesses were boycotted. In 1935 the Nuremberg Laws were passed by the German parliament. These laws stated that Jews were not German citizens, and could not vote in any elections. By 1939 Jews had been stripped of many basic human rights.

Kristallnacht

On the night of 9–10 November 1938, Germans attacked Jewish shops and synagogues. Over 100 Jews were killed. The night became known as *Kristallnacht* (Crystal Night or 'Night of Broken Glass') as the violence resulted in the streets being strewn with broken glass. The following year, Jewish professionals, for example doctors and lawyers, were stripped of their qualifications and lost their jobs. Jews began to be transported from Austria to Poland, and in 1941 all Jews had to wear a yellow Star of David (the symbol of the Jewish religion) on their clothes.

Ghettos

After 1939 many Jews tried to escape from Germany or German-occupied lands. Many of those who did not manage to escape were sent to live in ghettos. These were parts of towns or cities, often the slum areas, which were sealed off from the rest of the town or city. Jews were forced to live here in crowded conditions, often several families to one room. Many people died from disease or starvation. Other Jews died after being forced to work in terrible conditions. At times, Jews would be rounded up and moved from the ghettos into concentration camps. One of the most infamous camps was Auschwitz.

40

Source C

The perimeter fence and a watchtower at Auschwitz.

The Final Solution

Hitler was not content to strip Jews of their rights and their possessions. He wanted no Jews in Germany or indeed in Europe, and from 1941 he set about devising a plan to exterminate all Jews. This was known as the 'Final Solution'. Part of the Final Solution was to create extermination camps. Here, hundreds of thousands of Jews were sent to die. They were taken from their homes or from the ghettos without warning, loaded on to trucks or trains and transported to the camps. Any belongings of value were taken from them.

On arrival at the camps the Jews were split into groups. Families were separated. Some were sent to work; others who were sick, old or too young were sent straight to their deaths. The German officers told these people that they were being sent to take showers. They did not realise they were about to die. They were forced to undress and were put into shower chambers. The doors were then locked and gas was piped in through the shower heads. This killed everyone in the chamber within a few minutes. The dead were then either buried in mass graves or cremated. By 1944, around 12,000 people were killed like this every day. The Nazis took anything of value from the dead. Even their gold fillings were removed from their teeth and melted down.

In total, over six million Jews were killed by the Nazis. Those who were not killed in extermination camps were killed by murder units who travelled around the countryside. Others died of disease or starvation in the ghettos and camps, or were worked to death in appalling conditions in labour camps.

41

Anne Frank

One of the most famous Jews to have lived and died in a concentration camp was a young girl called Anne Frank. She is famous largely because she kept a diary about her life while hiding from the Nazis in occupied Holland. Anne died in the concentration camp at Bergen-Belsen, just before the camp was liberated by the Allies in 1945.

In 1933 Anne and her family moved from Germany to Holland to escape persecution. Many Jews thought Holland would be a safe refuge. The Frank family soon settled into life in Holland. This peace was shattered when the Nazis invaded Holland in 1940 and imposed their laws on the Dutch people. Anti-Jewish laws were brought in and life became more and more difficult for Jews. All human and civil rights were removed. In 1941 German police began arresting all the Jews in Holland. Otto Frank, Anne's father, arranged a secret hiding place for his family behind his office in Amsterdam, in a secret annexe. The family moved there in July 1942. Friends on the outside helped deliver food and supplies to them. Anne began keeping a diary of her experiences in the annexe.

On 4 August 1944 the Germans discovered the annexe and arrested the family. They were taken to Auschwitz, where Anne's mother died of starvation. Anne and her sister Margot were then taken to Bergen-Belsen camp.

Both caught typhus and died, one month before the end of the war and the liberation of the camp. Anne's father survived the Holocaust, and published her diaries which had been left behind in the annexe. Millions of people all over the world have now read her diaries and have learned about some of the horrors of the Holocaust through her eyes.

Questions

1. What does the word 'Holocaust' mean?

2. **a.** Why did Hitler persecute the Jews?
   b. What effect did the Nuremberg Laws have on Jewish people?

3. What was the Final Solution, and how did Hitler carry this out?

4. How useful is a source like Anne Frank's diary for telling us about persecution of the Jews in Holland? Explain your answer.

Extended writing

1. Think carefully about the life that Anne Frank must have had in hiding. Imagine that you are in her position and write a diary extract to explain and describe your new life in hiding.

42

Changes in Britain after the Second World War

The Second World War in Europe ended in May 1945. British people started asking questions about what the quality of life would now be like for them. During the war, they had pulled together and had shared with all levels of society. They had shared food, because of rationing. They had shared houses, because of evacuation and they had shared experiences like being bombed and sleeping in bomb shelters. However, people began to demand a better standard of living than they had before the war. They felt that they were entitled to a fairer and more equal world. The diets of poor people had actually improved during the war, as rations meant they suddenly were entitled to the same amount and variety of food as more wealthy people. They wanted this to continue after the war.

The events in Britain during the war had made a lot of people aware of the poverty in some parts of the country. During evacuation, children from inner cities were often moved to wealthy country areas to live with wealthier families. Many people from these families were shocked at how poor some of the evacuees were. Many of the children were not used to an inside toilet, running water, carpets and baths. They did not have many clothes and did not change or wash their clothes very often. Some children were infested with lice or suffered from infectious skin diseases.

Source D

Large numbers were infested with vermin, mainly head lice. One clinic shows that two-thirds of a party of 320 London children were infested with nits on arrival. Not only nits, but ringworm, impetigo, scabies and other skin problems.

A historian, RJ Cootes, commenting on the evacuees.

The Beveridge Report

The problems of poverty and poor health concerned many people, and the government began to take action. In 1942, Sir William Beveridge produced a report which outlined the problems for British people and what should be done to tackle them. In this report, he pointed out the 'Five Giant Evils' in society from which the public should be protected. These were:

- Want (poverty).
- Ignorance (lack of education).
- Disease (ill health).
- Squalor (living in poor conditions).
- Idleness (unemployment).

Source E

This cartoon from 1942 shows Beveridge tackling the first of the Five Giant Evils.

43

Beveridge wanted to get rid of these Evils and to make sure that every man, woman and child had enough food to eat, proper health-care and the opportunity for employment.

The report explained how this could be done. The British public was very impressed with the report. It gave them a goal to look forward to at the end of the war. It would make sure that people were cared for, as Beveridge said, 'from the cradle to the grave'. To do this, the government decided to set up a welfare state as soon as the war was over.

The welfare state

Ignorance

The first part of the welfare state was put in place in 1944. This was to deal directly with one of the Five Giant Evils – ignorance. The **1944 Education Act** stated the following:

- Secondary school education would be provided for all children.
- The legal school-leaving age would be raised to fifteen.
- Pupils would sit an eleven-plus exam.

Want

The **1945 Family Allowance Act** gave all families 5 shillings (25 pence) a week for each child born after the first child, up to the age of sixteen. Money for this would be paid to mothers or fathers through Post Offices.

Source F

▲ *One of the first mothers to collect Family Allowance money from the Post Office.*

The **1946 National Insurance Act** gave all workers sickness and unemployment benefit, maternity pay, and pensions for the elderly. This meant that even people who were not working would have an income.

Squalor

The government passed the **1946 New Towns Act** in an attempt to end the squalor that some people were living in and to provide homes for many of the people whose houses had been bombed in the war. New Towns were built in areas of the countryside away from large cities. Slums in inner cities were demolished and people were moved out to live in these New Towns, which had housing, schools, shops and leisure facilities. New Towns included East Kilbride and Glenrothes in Scotland, and Basildon and Stevenage in England.

Disease

In an attempt to improve the health of the British people, the government introduced the **1946 National Health Service Act**. This was driven by the Minister for Health, Aneurin Bevan, who overcame a lot of opposition and brought the Act into effect in 1948. This meant that free medical treatment was available to everyone. This included, at first, free spectacles, free dental treatment as well as free medical treatment.

Idleness

The Beveridge Report called upon the government to make sure that there were enough jobs available for all the people who wanted employment. Through investing in various industries, the government managed to create almost full employment by 1950. Imports were restricted and exports were encouraged. This helped to create demand for British-made goods, which meant that there were more jobs available in making them.

Questions

1. What events during the war made people want a fairer society after the war?

2. Explain in your own words each of the Five Giant Evils that Beveridge identified in his report.

3. Explain how each of the Five Giant Evils was tackled by the government.

Extended writing

1. Design a poster showing one of the changes which the government introduced after the war. You could add to the information above by searching on the Internet or visiting the library.

2. Write a report showing the good and the bad points of these changes introduced by the government. Think about the money and resources involved.

8

The Fifties and Sixties – civil rights in the USA

The 1950s and 1960s saw the formal advent of the civil rights movement in the USA. The Second World War gave black people a heightened awareness of the racism which existed in the USA. They had risked their lives fighting for their country, but when they returned home they remained second-class citizens.

The Ku Klux Klan

In the southern states of the USA black people were victimised by a secret terrorist organisation – the Ku Klux Klan (KKK) – that believed they were defending the 'American way of life' – that of white, Anglo-Saxon Protestant America. While the Klan had its origins in the mid-nineteenth century, it was revived in the 1920s and the persecution of black people continued well into the 1950s and 1960s.

Source A

Members of the Ku Klux Klan burning a cross in Polaski, Tennessee.

Source B

When the Constitution said all men are created equal, it wasn't talking about niggers.

A quote by JB Stoner, a racist white supremacist from Georgia.

Source C

Each time the Klan came on a raid they were led by police cars.

The writings of a campaigner for equal rights in the 1950s.

The Ku Klux Klan met at night and were disguised by their white, hooded garments (Source A). They were involved in lynching black people and used other forms of extreme violence towards them. They also dealt similarly with anyone who sympathised with the cause of black Americans. The KKK had members from all walks of life and many powerful men were members. To mark where they had met or had taken action they would burn a large wooden cross.

The struggle for equal rights

By the 1950s there was an increase in the demand by black people for change. They had been slowly gaining in political power in the late 1940s and by 1947 12 per cent of black people had registered to vote (compared to 2 per cent in 1940). Black people also became involved in trade unions. Progress, however, was slow. Not everyone was happy with this increasing status for black Americans, and brutal terror campaigns to dissuade black people from registering to vote continued, particularly in the South. Society was divided, with black people being segregated (kept separate) in all sorts of ways:

- Black employees were not allowed to use the same doors, toilets or canteens as fellow white employees.
- Some parks were reserved for white people only.
- Black people were not allowed to use the same theatres, cafés or water fountains as white people.
- On buses black people had to sit near the back of the bus and give up their seats (or get off the bus) to a white person if the bus was full.

The Montgomery bus boycott

In 1955 the case of Rosa Parks gained a lot of publicity. Rosa was travelling home from work in Montgomery, Alabama when she and other black people on the bus were asked to stand and let white passengers have their seats. Rosa refused and was arrested. This incident resulted in a boycott of all buses by black people. Among those refusing to travel on buses was a local preacher – Martin Luther King. During the boycott King was jailed and his house was bombed, but he kept urging black Americans to keep up this peaceful protest. The boycott had a huge effect on the bus company as more than 60 per cent of their travellers were black. In 1956 the company was forced to desegregate; white and black people could travel on equal terms.

Source D

Martin Luther King addressing a civil rights march in Washington, August 1963. ▶

Segregation in schools

In 1954 the Supreme Court of America declared that the segregation of white and black children in schools was illegal. While this law was passed in 1954 it took a lot longer to implement in some southern states of the USA.

In 1957 things came to a head in a place called Little Rock, Arkansas when nine black children wanted to attend the Central High School. The High School decided that they would accept the black students on 3 September 1957, not realising the reaction this would cause. The governor of Arkansas wanted to keep the school segregated despite the 1954 Supreme Court ruling, and used part-time soldiers from the local area to stop the black children from getting to the High School.

The US President (Eisenhower) became involved and ordered the governor to remove the troops. President Eisenhower also sent 1000 troops of his own in to protect the children. The troops remained there for a year. This incident gained a lot of publicity for the cause of black equality.

Source E

◀ *National Guard troops escort nine black students out of Central High School, Little Rock after demonstrations against integration, October 1957.*

The Montgomery bus boycott and the incident at Little Rock were not the only peaceful protests which made the headlines. Other planned protests involved black people going into cafés which refused to serve them (as they served only white people). This often led to violence between the staff and other customers and the activists. When the police intervened they arrested the activists.

By April 1960 this type of activity had spread all over the South and over 50,000 people took part in these protests. The media reported the events and many Americans were shocked at the violence being used against black people who had merely wanted the right to sit and have a cup of coffee.

Education was again to cause problems in 1962 when the Mississippi authorities prevented a black student, James Meredith, from going to university just because he was black. On Sunday 30 September 1962, 123 federal marshals, 316 American border patrolmen and 97 prison guards accompanied the black student to university. When they arrived there were over 2000 people waiting. Fighting began and two journalists were killed in the process. The president had to send in 16,000 troops to restore peace. The troops had to remain there for over a year to protect this one student.

Questions

1. Why do you think the war made black people more aware of their situation in the USA?

2. As the civil rights movement grew in the USA, what do you think happened to the Ku Klux Klan?

3. Why do you think the president became involved in the incident at Little Rock, Arkansas?

4. Imagine you were the President of the USA in 1962. What would you have done about the black student who wanted to go to university in Mississippi? Would you have sent in troops or not? Write a report to the Senate, explaining your actions and the reasons behind them.

5. Do you think it was sympathy for the black cause that made the bus company desegregate as a result of the Montgomery bus boycott? Explain your answer.

49

Martin Luther King

Martin Luther King was born on 15 January 1929. He was minister of a Baptist church in Montgomery, Alabama. He became involved in the Montgomery bus boycott of 1955 and was asked to be the chairman of the committee organising the boycott. His ability to grip his audiences with his passionate speeches became one of his most powerful weapons in the fight for civil rights for black people.

King formed the Southern Christian Leadership Conference (SCLC) in 1957. Deeply religious, his policies were always non-violent – he believed that peaceful demonstration would always win in the end.

In 1963 King organised a March on Washington in order to ask President Kennedy to do something for civil rights. In Washington, King made the most famous speech of the twentieth century in front of 200,000 people (Source F). It was televised and was to have a huge impact on the nation. A new law was written and presented to Congress; this was to be the 1964 Civil Rights Act.

Source F

I have a dream, that my little children will one day live in a society where they will not be judged by the colour of their skin but by the content of their character ... I have a dream that one day, down in Alabama, little black boys and little black girls will be able to join hands with little white boys and little white girls, as sisters and as brothers. I have this dream today.

Part of Martin Luther King's famous speech in Washington, 1963.

In 1964 the Civil Rights Act became law and all segregation laws were abolished. In 1964 King was awarded the Nobel Peace Prize. However, this did not end the struggle for race equality in the USA, and the work of King was not the only way ahead for many black people.

Four years after the passing of the Civil Rights Act, on 4 April 1968, King was murdered. He was shot as he stood on the balcony of a hotel in Memphis, Tennessee. He had gone there to support a strike by black dustmen. His killer, James Earl Ray, was a white racist. After the murder Ray was arrested, tried and spent the rest of his life in prison. When news of King's death broke out, there were many riots all over the USA. King's belief in non-violence was ignored, and 46 people were killed.

—— *Malcolm X*

In 1960 there had been a split in the civil rights movement. Many felt that non-violence, promoted by Martin Luther King, was not working. A new leader emerged – Malcolm X, who had a different view from King. Malcolm X was born in 1925 in Omaha, Nebraska. He was then called Malcolm Little. His family were treated very badly by white racists and were forced to move home several times to escape the violence. Malcolm X's father was murdered in 1931, and his mother was later committed to a mental institution. In 1938 he was expelled from school and sent to a detention centre. After being convicted of theft in 1945, he was sentenced to eight years in jail. It was while he was in jail that he discovered the faith that then changed his life – the Nation of Islam. This was a religious group that admitted only black Muslims.

Source G

We who are Muslims, followers of Elijah Muhammad, don't think that an integrated cup of coffee is sufficient payment for 310 years of slavery.

Malcolm X speaking in the 1950s.

50

The Nation of Islam rejected the ideas of integration and wanted nothing to do with white people. In 1950 Malcolm Little changed his name to Malcolm X. He did this because he felt that the name 'Little' was not his family's correct name. When black people had been slaves in America, they were not allowed their own surnames. They were often given the surname of their slave master. Many black people felt that to keep these names was a reminder of the days when white people ruled over black people. Until they could find out what their own family name had been before they were renamed by the slave masters, they decided to take on a letter of the alphabet. Malcolm chose the letter X.

Source H

Malcolm X. ▶

Malcolm X's policies were quite different from Martin Luther King's. He did not agree that black and white people should learn to live together peacefully. He felt that black people should remain separate from white people. He thought it was right to use violence in the struggle for civil rights.

In 1964 Malcolm X left the Nation of Islam, after he found out that the leader of the group was not sticking to the faith's strict moral standards. Later that year he met Martin Luther King for the first, and last, time. In February 1965, Malcolm X was killed by members of the Nation of Islam.

Source I

If they make the Ku Klux Klan non violent I'll be non violent. You get freedom by letting your enemy know that you'll do anything to get your freedom ... Fight them and you'll get your freedom.

Malcolm X speaking in 1965.

Questions

1. Why do you think Martin Luther King was always keen to get media publicity?

2. Make a timeline of all the non-violent incidents and protests in the USA from 1950 to 1964. Write a short comment next to each event.

3. Explain in your own words how Malcolm X's views were different from the views of Martin Luther King.

Extended writing

1. Write a report on the civil rights movement in the USA. Set your report out with a clear introduction, a list of points and a conclusion. In it you must mention segregation in schools and public places; voting; the Ku Klux Klan, Martin Luther King, Malcolm X and the Civil Rights Act of 1964. Use other sources to find out more information.

9

South Africa and human rights

In another part of the world there was a similar struggle against racism in the latter half of the twentieth century. This was taking place in South Africa.

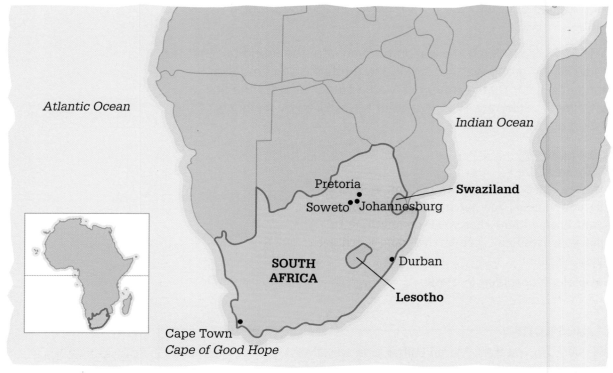

The location of South Africa. ▲

Apartheid

Apartheid means 'apartness'. It is the name given to the policy introduced by the ruling political party in South Africa in 1948 – the National Party, led by David Malan. The National Party won the General Election in 1948 and immediately set about using the policy of apartheid as a way of creating inequalities between white and black people. The white minority had found a way of keeping the wealth of the country for themselves. The law of apartheid classified people into categories:

- White people.
- Black people.
- Coloured people.
- Indian people.

Malan and his successors, including Dr Hendrick Verwoerd and John Vorster, ruthlessly enforced apartheid. As well as the apartheid laws, the Mixed Marriages Act and the Group Areas Act were introduced. The 1949 Mixed Marriages Act made marriages between people of different races illegal. The 1950 Group Areas Act confined black people to living in small pockets of land which made up only 14 per cent of the total land in South Africa.

There were over 23 million black people in South Africa and only 4.8 million white people. With the Group Areas Act millions of black people were forced by the government to move from their homes. They were forced to live in townships. These were poorly built and badly serviced areas of housing, found on the outskirts of large towns. Housing conditions were very basic, and the location of the townships meant that people had to travel huge distances to work. The most famous township was Soweto (short for South West Township) which was on the outskirts of Johannesburg.

Apartheid meant that black people were treated completely differently from white people. Black South Africans had to carry identity cards at all times. This was because of another law passed by the government – the 1952 Pass Book Act. The police would regularly stop black people and ask to see their identity cards, known as pass books.

Even though black and Asian South Africans did not agree with the laws and policies promoted by the National Party, they were unable to change the government as they were not allowed to vote. The government was deliberately going against the terms agreed in the Universal Declaration of Human Rights (see Source B on page 54).

Source A

▲ *A woman handwashing clothes in the township of Soweto, 1970.*

Source B

Article 3: Everyone has the right to life, liberty and security of person.

Article 6: All are equal before the law and are entitled without any discrimination to equal protection of the law.

Article 21: Everyone has the right to take part in the government of his country, directly or through freely chosen representatives.

Article 25: Everyone has the right to a standard of living adequate for health and well being of himself and his family, including food, clothing, housing and medical care....

Extracts from the Universal Declaration of Human Rights.

Source C

◀ *A taxi rank for 'whites only', Johannesburg, 1967.*

⎯ *The fight against apartheid*

Black South Africans were angry with the new laws which were being forced upon them. An organisation called the African National Congress (ANC), which had been formed in 1912, began to protest more strongly against discrimination. It tried to gain full citizenship for all South African citizens. When the ANC launched its Campaign for the Defiance of Unjust Laws in 1952, Nelson Mandela was elected National Volunteer in Chief. This was a campaign of mass civil disobedience. Black, Indian and coloured people began walking through entrances to public buildings which were reserved for 'Europeans Only'. They demanded service at 'Whites Only' counters at post offices, and they broke the Pass Laws.

Source D

◀ *Nelson Mandela (right) with ANC Secretary Walter Sisulu in 1952.*

Mandela travelled around South Africa organising resistance to apartheid. He was arrested and charged with organising this resistance, given a suspended sentence and prohibited from attending meetings or leaving Johannesburg. By the end of 1952 he was deputy president of the ANC. The next decade saw Mandela as the victim of oppression; he was banned from political activity, arrested and imprisoned.

On 21 March 1960 one of the most brutal events in South African history took place. The Pan African Congress (PAC), an anti-apartheid organisation, organised a protest outside Sharpeville police station against black people having to carry pass books. As a result the 5000 demonstrators were not carrying their pass books. The crowd was made up of men, women and children, all unarmed, but police started shooting at them, resulting in 69 black South Africans being killed and 186 wounded.

This marked the end of peaceful protests. The government banned the ANC and the PAC. Their leaders were tried and sentenced to imprisonment. In 1964 Mandela was imprisoned for life for encouraging a revolution.

The struggle against apartheid did not die with the arrest of the leaders of the ANC and PAC. Young people in the township of Soweto in the 1970s emerged as replacements, and would have the world watching events in South Africa. This new surge was inspired by Steve Biko.

Source E

Steve Biko. ▶

Steve Biko

Steve Biko was an ambitious man who was studying medicine at university and became active in black politics. He was expelled from university for his strong anti-apartheid beliefs. Biko led a group of young Africans against the apartheid system and set up the Black Consciousness movement to encourage black social and cultural development.

55

This movement influenced school children in the townships. In 1976 and 1977, many of them began organising demonstrations to protest about apartheid. The police and army responded to these protests using tear gas and gunfire, and many students were killed. In 1977 the Black Consciousness group was banned and Biko was arrested. He was so severely beaten by the police that he went into a coma and died. An inquest was held; it decided the police were not to blame, and claimed that Biko had battered himself against the cell wall and killed himself. Twenty years later, when major changes had been made in South Africa, five of the white policemen involved in Biko's arrest confessed to his killing. These confessions marked a change in attitude in South Africa – the whites were no longer above the law because of their jobs or their colour.

In 1986 the Pass Laws, which had been the cause of the Sharpeville protests, were finally removed, so that black South Africans no longer had to carry pass books. This was one of the reforms made by the government under Prime Minister PW Botha. He made a series of reforms, allowing black people limited freedom. As well as abolishing pass books, Botha encouraged black townships to elect their own local councils. He also abolished some forms of 'petty' apartheid – such as separate entrances, separate beaches, separate park benches and separate jobs for black people.

However, these reforms did not make life much different for many black South Africans. As a result, many anti-apartheid organisations pulled together and began attacking Botha's policies. These groups included many white South Africans who also wanted to see an end to apartheid. Violent demonstrations in townships led to more than 3350 people being killed between 1984 and 1988.

Nelson Mandela

Nelson Mandela was born in 1918. He trained as a lawyer. In 1943 he joined the ANC and began campaigning against apartheid. After the Sharpeville Massacre, Mandela launched a campaign to attack the country's economy. This included attacks on power stations and public buildings. Mandela was eventually arrested and was charged with sabotage and attempting to overthrow the government. In 1964 he was sentenced to life in prison, and was sent to Robben Island where he was kept in solitary confinement. He was not released until 1990, when President FW de Klerk lifted the ban on the ANC and released all political prisoners, including Mandela, who was then president of the ANC.

> **Source F**
>
> We want to touch him and say 'Here he is,' this man who has such a crucial role to play in the making of this new South Africa.
>
> *Desmond Tutu speaking on the release of Nelson Mandela in 1990.*

Mandela's release was followed in June 1990 with the abandonment of the Separate Amenities Act. This meant that both white and black people could use all public facilities such as cafés, libraries and shops. By the end of 1991 the Group Areas Act had gone, and the last parts of apartheid disappeared.

After his release Mandela still continued to strive to achieve the aims of democracy and harmony (see Source G). He has never wavered in his devotion to democracy, equality and learning. He has never answered racism with racism and his work has inspired thousands of people worldwide. His work was acknowledged in 1993 when he was presented with the Nobel Peace Prize on behalf of all the South Africans who had suffered and endured so much. In 1994, for the first time in South Africa's history, people of all races voted in the government elections. The ANC won 252 of the seats in government and Mandela became President of South Africa.

Source G

I have cherished the ideal of a democratic and free society in which all persons live in harmony and with equal opportunities. It is an ideal which I hope to live for and achieve. But if needs be, it is an ideal for which I am prepared to die.

On his release in 1990 Mandela made the same statement he had made at his trial in 1964.

Questions

1. Explain in your own words the term apartheid and the way it operated in South Africa.

2. What evidence is there to support the idea that the majority of white people in South Africa were in favour of apartheid?

3. Think carefully about the position of black people in South Africa after 1948. Write a report explaining the changes which had been made to their lives, and how these changes went against basic human rights. Start off by making a table listing the basic human rights, and next to each one list how the government of South Africa went against them.

4. **a.** What do you think was the intention behind the Campaign for the Defiance of Unjust Laws?
   b. What action did the government take as a result?

5. In what ways was Mandela victimised during the 1950s?

Extended writing

1. Write a report discussing the initial inquest into Steve Biko's death, and the turn of justice in 1997 when the white policemen confessed to his killing.

—— Scotland and apartheid

Throughout the world, there was opposition to the harsh regime of apartheid which had been created in South Africa. The United Nations condemned South Africa and many countries imposed sanctions on the country to try to force it to change its ways.

Source H

In the first decade of the twentieth century, a few years after the bitter Anglo-Boer war and before my own birth, the white-skinned peoples of South Africa patched up their differences and erected a system of racial discrimination against the dark-skinned peoples of their own land. ... The structure they created formed the basis of one of the harshest, most inhumane, societies the world has ever known. Now, in the last decade of the twentieth century, and my own eighth decade as a man, that system had been overturned forever and replaced by one that recognised the rights and freedoms of all peoples regardless of the colour of their skin.

An extract from **The Long Walk to Freedom,** *an autobiography which Nelson Mandela began writing in 1974, while in prison.*

In Britain, the opposition to apartheid took many forms. South Africa was forced to leave the Commonwealth. There were boycotts of South African goods and services. At the University of Glasgow, during the campaign for rector of the university, Chief Albert Luthuli was nominated. He was a chief of one of the main tribes in South Africa, the Zulu. He was elected but was unable to come to Glasgow to be installed as rector. The students of the university raised money to help students from South Africa come to Glasgow to study. In this way, they were showing their opposition to apartheid and their support for the struggle to end it.

There was also a boycott of sporting activities. South Africa was not allowed to take part in the Olympic Games or the Commonwealth Games and, within Britain, the government encouraged sporting organisations to have nothing to do with South Africa. In the 1970s, the English cricket team was due to tour South Africa. They had selected a player named Basil D'Olivera. The South African authorities refused to grant him access to the country since he was deemed to be a 'coloured' person under their race laws. The whole tour was abandoned in protest.

Source I

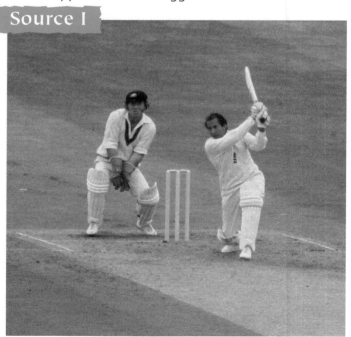

Basil D'Olivera, batting for England against Australia at Headingly, 1972. ▶

58

However, the South African rugby union team (the Springboks) was allowed to tour Britain in the early 1970s. There was great opposition to this tour and at every match there were demonstrations against the team and the system which they represented. At Murrayfield in Edinburgh, when Scotland played the Springboks, there was a huge anti-apartheid demonstration and the police had to hold back the crowds to prevent an invasion of the stadium. In addition, in 1975 the British Lions rugby team toured South Africa, despite immense pressure from the British government to cancel the tour. This was the last official South African tour of a British sporting team until the end of apartheid in the 1990s.

In Glasgow, the Council decided to take measures to embarrass the South African government. The street where the South African consulate was housed was renamed Nelson Mandela Place, so that anyone writing to the consul had to address letters to Nelson Mandela Place. In addition, the city fathers granted Mandela the freedom of the City of Glasgow. At the time, Mandela was unable to receive the honour in person, as he was still in prison on Robben Island. Petitions were also organised and demonstrations calling for Mandela's release and the abolition of the apartheid system were frequently held.

However, all of this opposition appeared, on the surface, to achieve nothing. Mandela remained in prison and apartheid seemed to be as strong as ever in South Africa.

Slowly, changes began to take place. The South African economy was suffering as a result of the boycotts and sanctions. South Africa was isolated from most of the world. Eventually the government began to accept that apartheid had to end and, step by step, South Africa began to be accepted by the rest of the world.

Questions

1. In Britain, opposition to apartheid took several forms.
   a. Describe three of these forms of opposition.
   b. Explain which of these would be most effective, and why.

2. How effective was the imprisonment of Nelson Mandela in preventing opposition to apartheid?

── *Change in the twentieth century*

At the start of a new century, there is a unique opportunity to look back and to measure how much has changed during the last 100-year period. Change is usually gradual and people living through it are often unaware of the changes taking place around them. Looking back, historians are able to identify what has changed. Their task is to try to explain why changes took place and the effect they had.

There were more changes in the twentieth century than in any previous century. Imagine life in 1800 and in 1900. Not a great deal changed between those times. Now imagine life in 1900 and in 2000. There has been a huge amount of change – in every country, for every person. Jobs, travel, communication, buildings, homes, health and society have all changed. Inventions such as computers and aeroplanes have meant that information, people and goods can move all over the world. Few areas of the world remain unexplored and every society has been affected in some way by change. The twentieth century saw two of the most horrific wars in history – the First and Second World Wars. Both wars resulted in huge changes for the countries and the people involved. The position of women changed dramatically in many countries, and civil rights for black people were finally upheld. Patterns in work and employment changed as never before and many countries accepted their responsibility to look after their people.

── *The end of the Empire*

At the start of the twentieth century, Britain ruled supreme. It was said that the Sun never set on the British Empire. Given that the Empire was spread throughout the world, that was probably true. However, the twentieth century has seen all of the former European colonial powers give up much of their empires.

In Britain's case, the rights of its colonies had already been recognised by the establishment of dominion status in Canada, New Zealand and Australia during the nineteenth and early twentieth centuries. This trend to give more freedom and responsibility to countries of the Empire was accelerated after the Second World War. First India and then Pakistan were granted independence in 1947. Later, Britain's colonies in Africa became independent. Gradually all of Britain's colonies were released from the Empire. Britain is now an important member of the Commonwealth, in which all countries are regarded as equal.

Source A

▲ *Queen Elizabeth and other delegates at the Commonwealth Heads of Government meeting in Coolum, Australia, March 2002.*

This change in the position of Britain has also been reflected in relations with Europe. One hundred years ago, Britain tried to keep out of European affairs as far as possible. However, two World Wars have shown that this is not a realistic position. In 1973 Britain joined the European Economic Community (now called the European Union).

61

Government in Britain

In terms of politics, the greatest change in Britain came about in 1900–2000. In 1900, the government in Westminster in London made decisions for the whole of the country and the Empire. In 1999, Parliaments for Scotland and Northern Ireland and a National Assembly for Wales were set up. Now Scotland has a more direct say in the matters which concern it most – health, education, economic development and social welfare.

Source B

The setting up of the Scottish Parliament marked the high point of attempts since the mid-nineteenth century to have devolution of power from Westminster (Source B). Whether there will be any further constitutional change in the twenty-first century is open to speculation.

Queen Elizabeth opening the Scottish Parliament, 1 July 1999. ▶

— *Social changes*

The greatest change in Scotland has probably been in social terms. In 1900 the classes were strictly divided, with the rich enjoying all the privileges of life. The middle classes were trying to copy the upper class, within their limited budgets, and the working classes were struggling to maintain an acceptable standard of living. However, throughout the twentieth century, the government has accepted the need to provide help for all members of the community.

Again, the catalyst of change has been war. In 1919 Prime Minister Lloyd George had promised 'a land fit for heroes' for the soldiers returning from fighting in the First World War. The reality for these soldiers was very different and many who had served their country in the war felt betrayed. They were not met with a land fit for heroes, instead they were faced by poor housing, unemployment and the lack of opportunity.

During the Second World War the coalition government produced a report which highlighted the social problems in Britain and set out how these might be solved. The Beveridge Report promised to tackle the 'Five Giant Evils' which it identified as the causes of the problems in Britain – ignorance, disease, want, idleness, and squalor (see page 43). The report led the way for the completion of the welfare state, the benefits of which all who live in Britain continue to enjoy.

During the twentieth century, the social classes saw the strict divisions between them dissolve. In addition, within class groupings, there were great improvements and people became more equal. No longer are workers regarded as unimportant in their places of employment. The progress of trade unions and the rights of all union members have been important features of the twentieth century.

Equally important was the change in status of women, who were considered the weaker sex in 1900. It was a long, hard and often frustrating campaign but gradually the position of women in society improved. Perhaps the best example of this was the success of Margaret Thatcher in becoming Britain's first female Prime Minister. However, all women have seen improvements in their lives helped by changes in public opinion. This came about due to the effects of female contributions in the two world wars.

Another social change was the growth in the diversity of the people choosing to live in Scotland. Since 1945 the Society of Scotland has benefited from the arrival of people from countries of the former Empire and other countries. No High Street in Scotland would be complete without its share of stores and restaurants servicing these diverse cultural groups.

Economic changes

Economically, the position of Britain and Scotland altered dramatically during the twentieth century. At the start of the twentieth century, British industry ruled supreme and Scotland prospered as part of that world economy. The domination of Clyde shipyards was unchallenged and Scotland's heavy industries – coal, iron, steel and marine engineering – all serviced this industry. However, since the Second World War, these traditional industries have declined in relative importance to the Scottish economy. They have been replaced by the computer industries of 'silicon glen' and the service industries of call centres, banking and financial services.

Source C

A call centre, Edinburgh, September 2000. ▲

In 2000, the world looked forward to a new millennium. What would it bring?
The pace of change accelerated throughout the twentieth century so much that
the possibilities for the future seemed endless. Who could be without the car, the
mobile phone, the Internet and the high standards of living enjoyed by many
people around the world? The challenge facing Scotland and the rest of the world
is this – how do we continue to enjoy the benefits of modern life without
destroying the environment and, more importantly, how do we share these benefits
equally? This is the inheritance that the children of the world have for their future.

Questions

1. Select one major event or person of the
   twentieth century. Explain the short and
   long term effect of this/him/her on society.

2. What were the major changes in
   government within the twentieth century?

3. Describe the effects of the First and
   Second World Wars on:
   a. the role of women
   b. work and employment.